First published 1980 by
Octopus Books Limited
59 Grosvenor Street
London W1

© 1980 Octopus Books Limited

ISBN 0 7064 1357 1

Produced by Mandarin Publishers Limited
22a Westland Road, Quarry Bay, Hong Kong

Printed in Hong Kong

Educational and Series advisor Felicia Law

Animal ABC

illustrated by
Peter Woolcock

octopus

aA

armadillos acting

b B

bears bathing

c C

cats crying

d D

dogs driving

e E

elephants eating

fF

foxes flying

g G

goats gardening

hH

hippos hurrying

i l

iguanas invading

j J jaguars jogging

k K kangaroos kicking

l L

lions laughing

m M

monkeys
making mischief

nN
nightingales
nursing

oO
ostriches
ogling

p P

penguins parading

q Q quails quivering

r R rabbits running

START

s S

squirrels storing

tT

tigers tobogganing

u U   unicorns in uniform

v V   voles visiting

VOLE TOURS
OVERSEAS VISITORS

w W

walruses washing

x X excited oxen

y Y yaks yelling

z Z zebra zig-zagging